Saltwater Fly-Casting Techniques

Also by Lefty Kreh

Longer Fly Casting

Fly Casting in Salt Water

Practical Fishing Knots

Fishing the Flats

Fly Casting with Lefty Kreh

Saltwater Fly Patterns

Advanced Fly Fishing

Lefty's Little Library

Presenting the Fly

101 Fly-Fishing Tips

Solving Fly-Casting Problems

The L.L. Bean Saltwater Fly Fishing Handbook

Saltwater Fly-Casting Techniques

How to Cast Effectively for the Biggest Fish
and Under the Most Demanding Situations

Lefty Kreh

Illustrations by Rod Walinchus

The Lyons Press

An Imprint of the Globe Pequot Press

The Lyons Press is an imprint of the Globe Pequot Press.

Printed in the United States of America

2 4 6 8 10 9 7 5 3 1

Library of Congress Cataloging-in-Publication Data is available on file.

CONTENTS

INTRODUCTION

Fly casting in salt water is more difficult to master than fly casting in fresh water. Small brooks, streams, larger rivers, and freshwater lakes are often protected from the wind, and in many situations, long, accurate casts are seldom required. Trout anglers try to get as close as possible to a fish before they cast, and good presentations can be difficult when fishing nymphs, streamers, or dry flies with a long line.

These flies are generally smaller than those used in saltwater fishing, and even weighted freshwater flies are light when compared with many of the patterns commonly used in saltwater fly fishing. And the rod sizes match these conditions: In most freshwater fly fishing situations, rod weights of 3 to 8 are common, but in saltwater fly fishing, rods generally range from sizes 8 to 12.

Although speed and accuracy are helpful when fly fishing in fresh water, they are absolutely crucial when fly fishing in salt water. When fishing for trout, you can locate a fish, observe it, and determine what it is feeding on before offering it something. A good trout fisherman will take a sample of the insects drifting in the water column, select a fly to match the hatch, and cast their offering to the fish. All of this takes time. While fishing in fresh water, I've often taken ten minutes to relocate myself because a cast might be impossible, or I determined that

I would have difficulty landing a fish, all while the fish continued to feed.

In many saltwater situations you have a maximum of five to eight seconds to get the fly to the fish, and if you don't throw it far enough or accurately on your first cast, you may miss the opportunity. The first cast is the most important in all fly fishing, but I've watched anglers cast perhaps ten times before they put the fly where it would drift correctly to a trout. You simply don't get ten chances when offering a fly to a saltwater fish; an example would be when your companion or guide poles you across a saltwater flat where bonefish, permit, stripers, or tarpon are difficult to see. Many times, you won't spot the fish until you're only yards away from it. Unless you can make an almost instant and accurate cast, you're not going to catch that fish. Another example is when you'll see a school of fish breaking on the surface as you're cruising inshore or offshore waters. You must be ready to cast the moment your boat arrives at the scene, and more often than not that first cast will have to be very long. And when fishing on open salt water where no fish may be evident, you'll need to make extended retrieves to present the fly to as much water as possible. This requires long casts with shooting heads, and they demand a special casting technique.

None of this should deter you from taking up saltwater fly fishing, but be aware that you have to be a much better caster in salt water than you do in fresh water. The purpose of this book is to help you get to the next skill level and solve the problems you'll encounter when fishing in salt water, none of which are too difficult. There are other differences between saltwater and freshwater fly casting, and I'll describe the tricks and techniques you'll need in order to fish effectively. You'll find that not only will these techniques expand your repertoire—whether you're fishing in fresh water or salt—but you'll be able to catch a wider variety of larger fish under the most demanding situations.

1

Unlearning Bad Habits

Every fly fisherman would like to cast better, but why is it sometimes difficult to either understand or perform well? I like to think that much of the difficulty comes from when fly fishing became a serious pursuit, several centuries ago in Europe. Most anglers fished on relatively small streams no more than a few yards across, and the tackle of the day was a very long rod (12 to 16 feet long) made of locally available wood. A very short fly line was constructed by twisting together the hairs from a horse's tail. With such a long rod and short line it was only necessary to lift the rod to a vertical position and return it to a near-horizontal position. Since the line/rod combo was constant, only one casting motion was required.

As the equipment evolved, instructors began to teach the fly-casting stroke by relating it to the hands on a clock face, and this concept has persisted to this day. Most books, magazine articles, and videos teach that certain casting motions should be performed at a position on a clock face, and I think that this is why most fly fishermen don't cast as well as they could. I believe that if we eliminate casting stroke positions as related to the clock face everyone could better understand fly casting and become better casters.

2

What Is Fly Casting?

Fly casting can be explained pretty easily without getting into physics and technical language. The basic cast—whether forward or backward—is a gradual acceleration of the rod, which pulls against the weight of the line and causes the rod to flex or load. At the final moment of the cast (again, whether forward or backward) the rod tip is greatly accelerated and then stopped. This causes the line to *unroll* in the direction of the target or away from the target, and the more efficiently you can unroll the line the easier the cast. It's a good idea to remember that a backcast is simply a forward cast in the opposite direction—so the same principles apply to both.

Fortunately, good casting does not require strength and any lady or older person can cast well. In all the years I've taught fly casting lessons, I've found that women usually learn faster. I think that because they don't have great strength, they learn to rely on proper technique instead of trying to muscle their way out of problems.

BASIC FLY CASTING PRINCIPLES

Although a fly rod may seem magical when some people cast, great casting doesn't involve a magician or a magic wand. Several basic principles govern what happens when you cast a fly line, and they apply to all casts regardless of the method you use. Understanding the following principles will almost certainly make anyone a better caster.

1. If you are right-handed, the right foot should be positioned to the rear and the left foot should be slightly forward. Lefties should do the reverse.

2. Before you can load the rod, you must remove the slack from the line. Loading a rod requires line tension against the tip, so that when you move the rod, the weight of the line holds the rod tip back, causing the rod to bend. You wouldn't try to cast a spinning lure before reeling the lure close to the rod tip to eliminate slack. It's the same with fly casting.

3. Once the slack is gone, the only way to load the rod is to move the casting hand with ever-increasing speed to a sudden stop. The cast is one continuous acceleration, with the slowest movement at the beginning of the stroke and the fastest just before the stop. The more you can accelerate the rod tip and the shorter the stop at the final moment of the cast, the tighter the casting stroke and the faster and farther the

line will travel. If the rod hand moves ever faster during the stroke, the rod will continue to bend further. If the rod hand doesn't speed up or slows, the rod will lose part of its bend and won't load properly.

4. When the rod hand stops, the rod will straighten and the fly line will follow the direction of the rod tip when the rod tip becomes fully unloaded. This determines casting direction and is the key to accuracy. It's like shooting a rifle; the gun can be pointed in any direction before the trigger is pulled, but the bullet will only travel in the direction of the barrel at the instant where the trigger was pulled. On a fly cast, the stop at the end of the speed-up-and-stop is like pulling the trigger on a rifle, and the line will follow the direction of the rod tip when the rod tip stopped. There is no way around this, and to determine direction you have to decide where you want the line to go *before* you stop the rod. Once the rod tip stops, *you can't change the direction of the cast.* Understanding this will allow you to improve your accuracy and make several different casts, such as the curve cast.

5. The thumb should rest along the length of the rod throughout the cast and should point directly toward the target, regardless of whether this is ahead of you on the forward cast or behind you on the backcast. This optimizes the transmission of energy at the end of the cast, and more importantly, it improves accuracy. The rod tip will follow the thumb, the line will follow the rod tip, and the fly will

follow the line. This is where the sidearm cast I advocate is so important. If you cast directly overhead with the common clock method, your wrist will naturally twist outwards as it nears the vertical position on the backcast. As your wrist twists, your thumb will point outwards and away from the target. This takes energy away from the cast and makes the cast less accurate for three reasons. First, you're throwing the line in a wide loop. Second, your forearm can't extend behind you during a backcast by the time it gets in a vertical position (try demonstrating this with a vertical cast and a sidearm cast). Finally, it is more difficult to cast when your wrist and thumb are twisted outward. Demonstrate this by casting back and forth with your knuckles pointed away from you. Now try it with your thumb behind the rod and your knuckles toward the target on the forward cast. It's a subtle, but crucial point: use a sidearm cast and point the thumb directly toward the target on the forward cast and the backcast.

6. The longer the distance over which the rod and arm travel during the cast (whether forwards or backwards), the easier it is to make the cast. The converse is equally true: the shorter the casting stroke, the harder you have to work to put the same load in the rod. Think of it this way: In order for the line to unroll effectively, you have to accelerate the line to a certain speed. It's difficult to build that speed up if your cast goes through a quarter of a circle; it's constricted. It's easier to build up the necessary load if the casting arm and the rod are able to go through a longer stroke that begins directly in front of you and ends directly behind you with a very quick speed-up-and-stop. When you have to cast farther or cast into the wind, don't cast harder, cast smarter by lengthening your stroke.

7. The elbow should remain at one height throughout the cast, and the proper height of the elbow is at its regular resting height. As a demonstration, let your arm rest naturally at your side, then raise your forearm and imagine that it's resting on a shelf. That's the correct elevation for your elbow, and although your elbow can move forward and backwards, it should remain in this plane—in contact with the imaginary shelf, if you like—throughout the cast. The angle of the backcast is determined by the angle that the rod hand stops, but the elbow should not be elevated. If you elevate your elbow, the energy of the cast follows the elbow as it flops around, which results in wide, inefficient, unmanageable tailing loops instead of tight, efficient, and accurate loops.

These principles apply to every cast, and everyone must cast according to them regardless of their individual style. How far you move your hand, the direction you move your hand, how fast you move your hand, may all change; in fact, they must change for different fishing situations. But these principles are invariable. They have no exceptions. Even though rules or instructions that don't take these principles may work in a limited way in some applications, those rules and instructions will often leave you frustrated when fishing conditions change.

Fly casters who try to cast precisely by moving their rod between two predetermined clock points know the helpless feeling of trying to throw a heavily weighted fly, hitting themselves in the back with a fly, catching a tree on their backcast, or tangling lines on the forward cast. This is because the casters are following instructions that are suited to a different set of conditions. If you focus on the principles behind your movements you will be able to correct your faults and make casts you thought were impossible.

3

Techniques for Saltwater Fly Casting

THE DOUBLE HAUL

Next to mastering the proper casting stroke, the double haul is the most important tool a fly caster can learn. It permits you to throw a longer line, cast against the wind, and present heavier flies and lines with less effort. Once you master the double-haul, you can use it to some degree on almost every cast. But before we examine how to double haul properly, I'll describe some fly casting basics that pertain to the double haul.

1. You don't cast a fly line as you would a lure. Instead, a fly line unrolls. Once the line has unrolled and straightened at the end of a cast, it will go no farther, and will begin to fall.

2. All casting strokes are divided into two parts; a relatively long motion in which the rod is gradually accelerated, ending with a much faster and shorter speed-up-and-stop of the

tip. The speed-up-and stop is often referred to as a power stroke, but it's really a speed stroke.

3. The shorter the distance the rod tip travels during the speed-up-and-stop, the tighter the loop will be. The faster the rod tip accelerates during the speed-up-and-stop, and the more abruptly it stops, the faster the line will travel.

When using the double haul, as with most casts, the first portion of the back or forward cast is a relatively long sweeping of the rod. This causes the rod to flex or load. If you release the line in your hand at the end of the sweep it will travel only a short distance. But if you complete the second portion of the cast—a brief, fast, speed-up-and-stop of the rod tip—the line will go a considerable distance. And the shorter and faster the tip moves during that speed-up-and-stop, the farther the line will unroll. Remember this because it will help make you a better double hauler.

Almost every angler can improve his or her double haul if we relate the speed-up-and-stop of the rod tip to the motion of the haul. The motion of the haul should reflect the speed-up-and-stop of the rod. Most fishermen haul on the line at a continuous speed through the backcast and again through the forward cast, and the effect is the same as if the rod is swept back and forward with the rod hand instead of employing the speed-up-and-stop.

Like the rod stroke, the most efficient haul consists of two parts. There is a relatively long, slow pull on the line that mirrors the rod's first segment of the cast. When the rod speeds up and stops, the hauling hand should simultaneously speed up and stop with an action that mirrors the rod. This dramatically increases the line speed and the efficiency of the cast. If the two events don't occur simultaneously, the speed and efficiency suffers.

There are also other disadvantages to making a long, continuous pull. Anglers who make a long, continuous pull on the backcast often have a lot of slack line when they start the forward cast. This slack must be removed before an effective forward haul can begin, and the slack line can get snagged behind the rod handle. Also, the distance that the rod tip moves during the speed-up-and-stop determines loop size. If you make a short speed-up-and-stop with the rod hand, then continue a long, slow haul, the tip won't stop, but will continue to flex and load past the end of the stroke, which will result in a large, inefficient loop.

MASTERING THE ROLL CAST

With the exception of the conventional overhead cast, the roll cast is utilized more than any other. It's beneficial in a wide variety of fishing situations, and downright necessary in others. It is used most frequently when there is little or no room for a backcast, but you can also use it to lift a popping bug or fly silently from the water. Another occasion would be when the fly is snagged on something; a roll cast will put the line beyond the snag, and then you can make a backcast to free the fly. When wading the bonefish flats I often keep about 20 feet of line plus leader outside the rod tip. As I move along, I roll cast to keep the line out in front of me so that if I see a target, the line is ready for a quick backcast. If you're fishing with a fast sinking line or lead-core shooting head, the roll cast is vital in lifting the line from the deep so you can make an effective backcast.

Given that this is one of the most useful casts a fly fisher can have in their arsenal, it's surprising that almost no one makes an efficient roll cast. I think that this is because most instructors teach what I regard to be poor technique, which only complicates the problem of learning this useful and easy cast. To deliver a good roll cast, we have to remember some simple but important fly casting concepts.

The most important factor to remember is that you are *only modifying the forward cast.* Instead, most fly fishermen modify the entire cast. When roll casting only the backcast is modified. If you already know how to make a good forward cast, you can make an effective roll cast.

The second thing to remember is that in any cast, the line will follow the direction of the rod tip when the tip speeds up and stops.

The third thing we should keep in mind is that the size of the loop is determined by the distance the rod tip moves during the speed-up-and-stop. The speed-up-and-stop occurs after the rod moves forward. The size of the loop is almost exactly the same as the vertical distance the rod tip drops during the speed-up-and-stop. For example, if your rod tip drops two feet on the speed-up-and-stop, the diameter of the loop will be two feet.

Lastly, the longer the cast before the speed-up-and-stop, the easier it is to make the cast. Watch great casters: When they need distance, they manage to get the rod well behind them. They've learned that the farther the rod tip moves during the cast, the farther and easier the fly and line go.

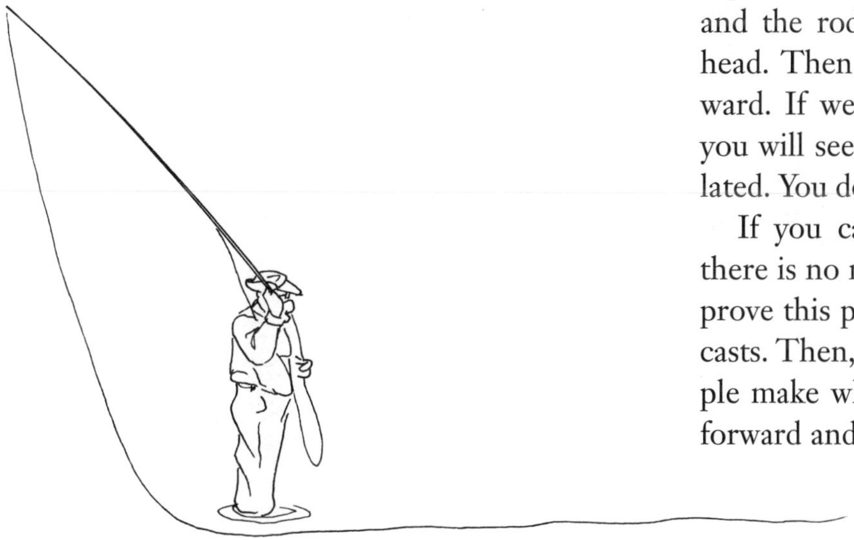

THE CONVENTIONAL INEFFICIENT ROLL CAST

This is how the typical fly fisherman makes a roll cast. The rod is brought up until the rod is pointing at a near vertical angle. The elbow is elevated and the rod hand is near the top or above the head. Then the rod is swept forward and downward. If we examine the four important points, you will see that all of the factors have been violated. You don't want to modify your forward cast.

If you can make a good forward cast, then there is no reason to alter that. Try something to prove this point. Make several conventional false casts. Then, make the forward cast that most people make when roll casting by sweeping the rod forward and downward. The energy of the cast is

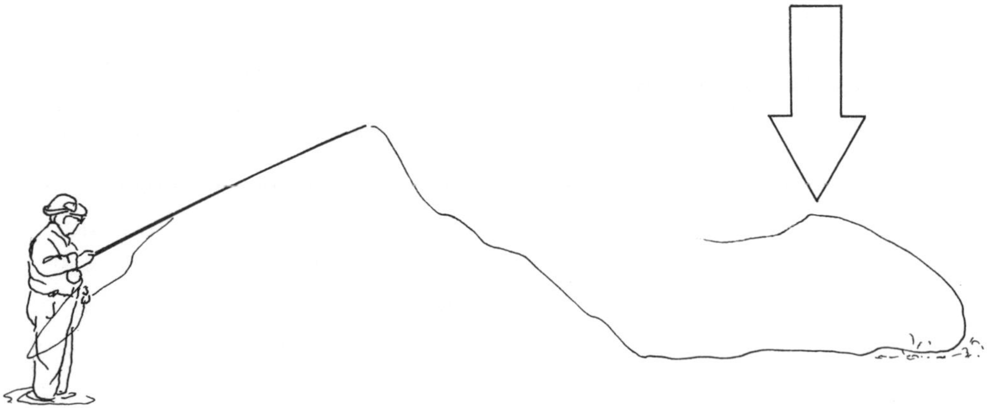

thrown around a wide loop and the fly will dive to the surface in front of you. The line and fly go in the direction you stop the rod tip. Most people end the roll cast by driving the tip at the water in front of them. That's the reason why the line usually falls in a heap in front of them.

In summary, if the rod begins the cast from a near vertical position it doesn't offer much assistance on the cast. With an elevated elbow and high hand, the fly fisherman is forced to bring the rod forward and downward in a long, sweeping motion. The size of the loop is determined by the distance that you speed up and stop the rod tip at the end of the cast. And, the line goes in the direction the rod tip stops. Most people begin a roll cast with the rod tip held at a vertical angle and then sweep forward and downward. Anyone doing this is forcing the rod to throw the largest line loop possible and drive the fly into the water in front of him or her.

THE EFFICIENT ROLL CAST

It's really very easy to improve your roll cast, and here's how to do it. Slowly bring the rod as far back as fishing conditions will permit. The ideal situation would be to have the rod tip pointing directly behind you and away from the target. It is very important that you don't raise your rod hand above your shoulder when moving the rod back; instead, the rod hand should be at about the belt level. Then stop the rod for just an instant. This allows the surface tension of the water to grip the line, and you'll use this surface tension to load or flex the rod as you make your forward cast. If you don't allow the line to stop, the rod won't load properly because it has nothing to pull against, and the forward cast will be weakened.

After the line stops, start to make a normal forward cast. Your elbow should remain on the imaginary shelf and your rod hand should remain at the same height throughout the forward cast. If

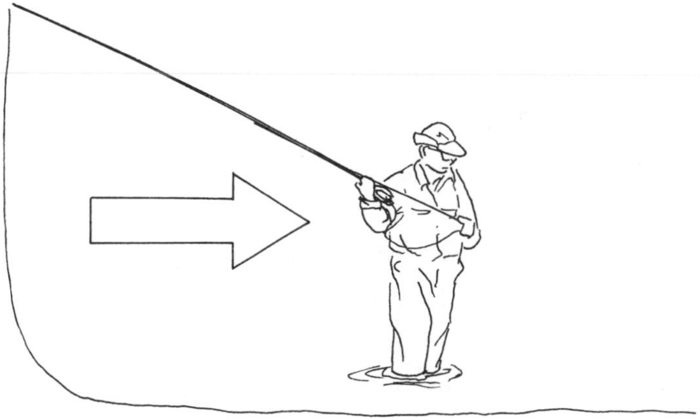

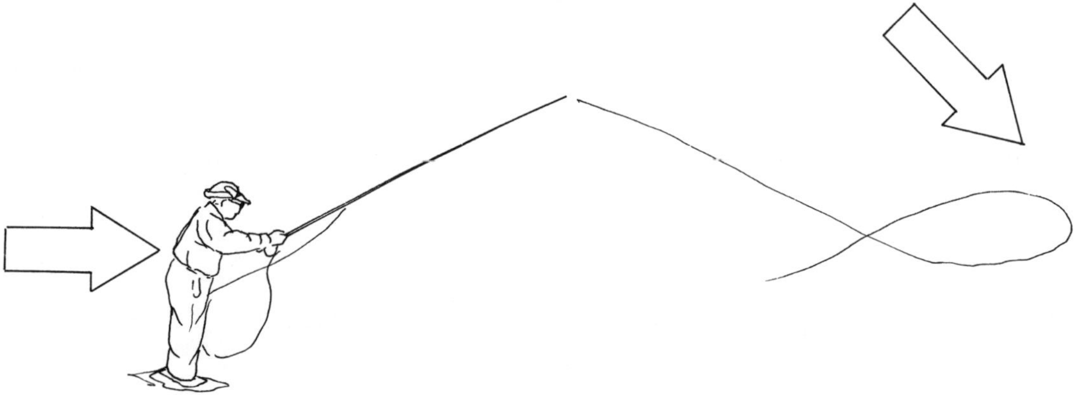

your rod hand travels upwards you'll make a large, inefficient loop. If your rod hand travels downwards, the line will pile up in front of you, as with the inefficient roll cast above. But if you make a normal forward cast with the hand moving straight ahead, you will be directing almost all of the energy in the cast toward the target. A good roll cast will have a line loop that resembles this one—or a good forward cast loop.

Again, if the rod travels a short distance during the speed-up-and-stop and the rod tip stops quickly, you will be able to attain a tight loop and a long cast. This is as true for the roll cast as for any good forward cast.

CASTING ACCURATELY WITH A SIDE WIND

It's very difficult to make a cast when the wind blows at a right angle to the fly fisherman. What usually happens is that the angler sees a fish just as a heavy breeze blows from the left. The angler makes the cast, but the wind acts against the line and leader and blows the fly yards to the right of the fish. As a result, the angler misses an opportunity to catch his quarry.

If we analyze why the line and fly are blown off target, we can make adjustments so that an accurate cast is possible in all but the strongest side winds. To make an accurate cast we need to do only a few simple things. First, it's important to realize that you shouldn't try to shoot additional line; you can make an accurate cast only when you have the correct amount of line necessary to reach the target. Secondly, the line, leader, and fly always travel in the direction that the rod tip speeds up and stops. If we direct the cast someplace above the water, the breeze can push it downwind. In addition, once the rod tip goes through the final speed-up-and-stop on the forward cast, the direction cannot be changed.

To make an accurate cast when the wind is blowing from the side, it is vital that you direct the cast at the target so that the line, leader, and fly travel to the target. Once the rod tip goes through the final speed-up-and-stop, immediately drop the rod tip to the water's surface. The line will unroll directly on the water where it can't be blown sideways and will lead straight up to the target.

The angler directs the fly line well above the water. Throughout the cast the wind will be pushing the line, leader, and fly sideways to the target.

If the rod is then lowered, the wind continues to drive the line/leader and fly downwind of the target, and an inaccurate cast results.

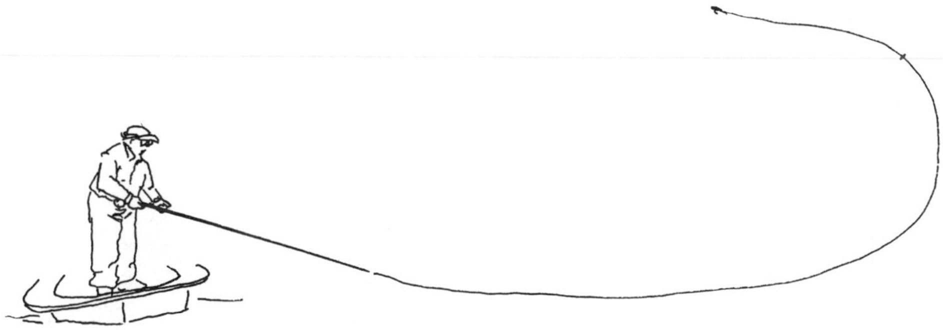

The angler will shoot no line and aims the cast directly at the target.

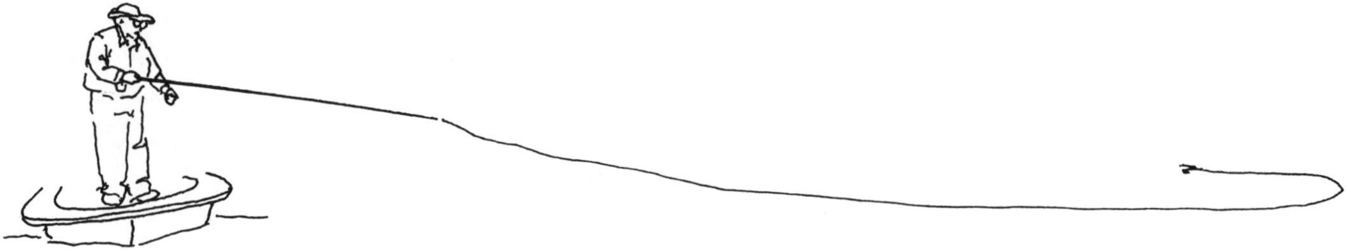

It is important immediately after the rod tip stops to lower the tip to the water. This will lay all of the fly line on the water as the cast unrolls. Since the wind cannot affect it, the cast can be made accurately, even in a strong side wind.

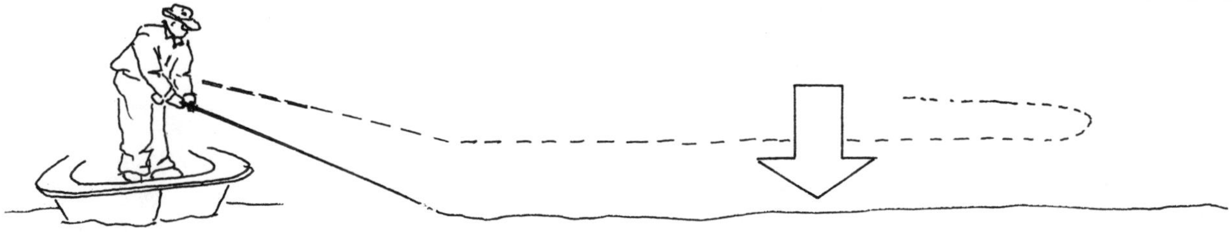

HOW TO CAST WHEN THE WIND IS BEHIND YOU

You can make a very long forward cast if the wind is coming from behind you, but only if you make a good backcast. First, make a relatively low backcast to the side.

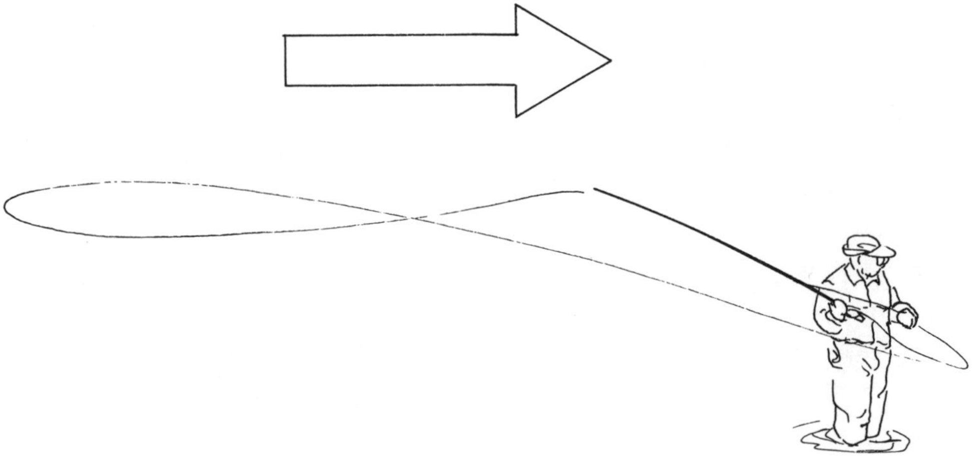

If you throw the line much higher than normal on the forward cast, the wind will pick it up like a kite, and you can make a long cast.

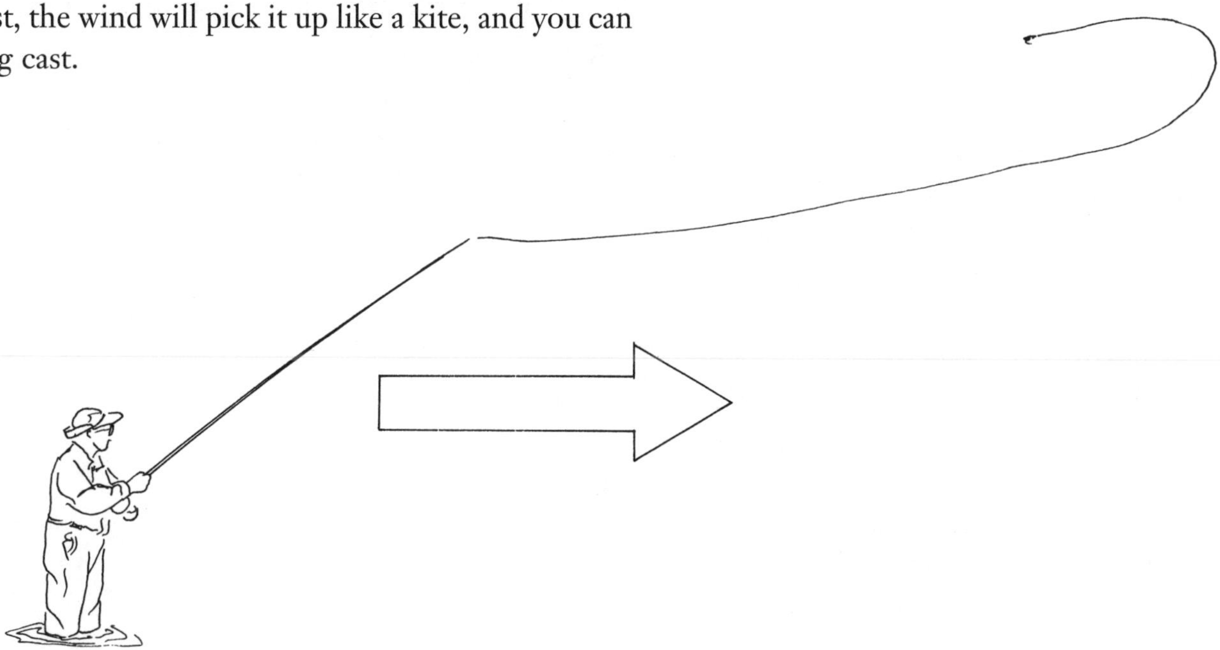

CASTING WHEN THE WIND IS ON YOUR RIGHT

Fly fishermen have been plagued by wind that comes from the casting side; for right-handers, that's a wind that blows from right to left. As the angler follows through on a forward cast, the line and fly are blown toward the caster, which may endanger the caster or an angling companion if the two happen to be on a boat. Some right-handed fly fishermen try to get around this problem by holding the arm at a 45-degree angle to the left—across the chest—to keep the fly line downwind. But this restricts rod motion, which reduces your ability to make a long cast. What you need to do is make a cast with a long, full extension that keeps the fly and the line away from you as you cast.

The following illustrations show how to do this. First, remember that you shouldn't raise your elbow; instead, you should keep it on the imaginary shelf. If you raise the elbow while making the backcast, you tend to make a large loop on the forward cast.

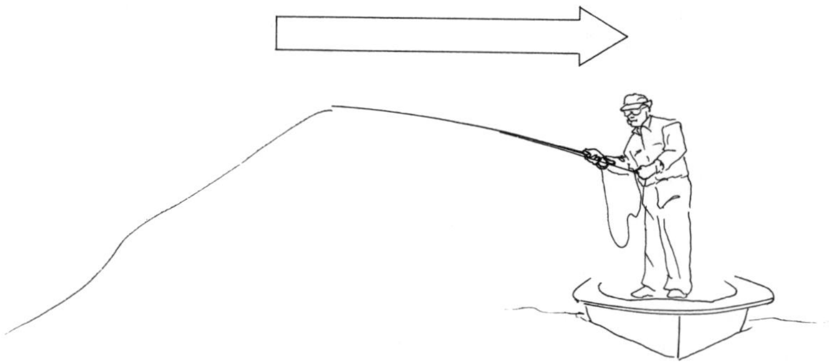

Make the backcast well to the side. If you make the backcast properly, the line will be carried far enough upwind so that the fly won't strike you as you complete the backcast. Note that the elbow has been kept in its normal low position throughout the backcast.

On the forward cast, the elbow should be maintained at the same height and the rod should be tilted slightly to the downwind side of the angler throughout the cast. The action of the wind and of tilting the rod will cause the line and the fly to travel downwind from the angler, out of harm's way. At the end of the forward cast the rod tip should speed up and stop straight ahead. It's important to avoid dipping the rod tip at this point, which would pull the loop open and reduce the distance of your cast.

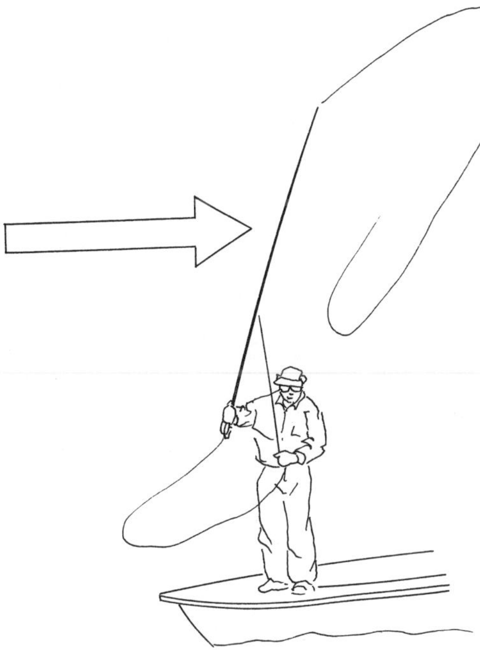

HOW TO CAST WHEN THE WIND IS COMING TOWARD YOU

One of the most common problems encountered in saltwater fly fishing is that the wind will come toward you as you cast and make it impossible to cast the line forward. A sinking line will penetrate the breeze because it is thin and it has more weight, but more often than not you'll have to use a floating line.

The wind resists the line as it unrolls, straightens, and falls when an angler casts the line at a normal angle and height—about eye level or slightly above. The result is that the line falls short of the target.

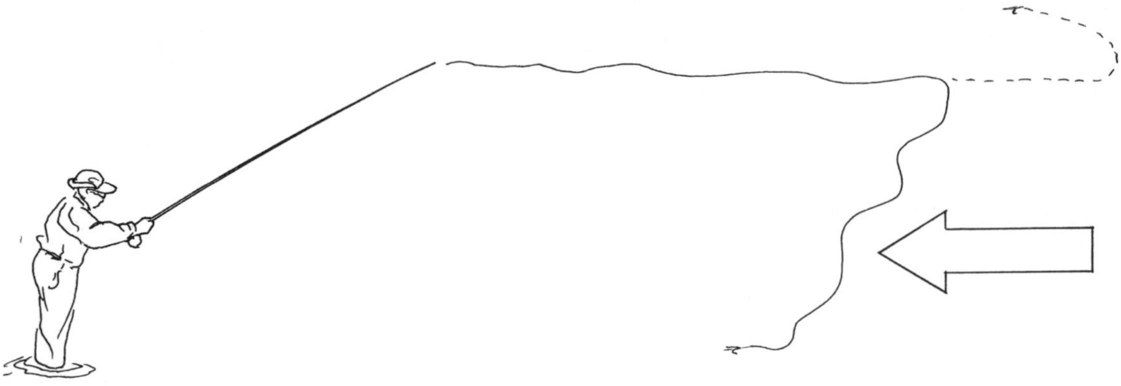

If the angler directs the cast to the target so that the fly touches the surface the moment the line completely unrolls, the fly and line won't be blown backwards. This is one of the few instances when the angler should direct the cast to hit the target instead of above the target.

Another important factor is that if you overpower the rod, you'll destroy the loop. You'll be able to penetrate the wind much better if you make a tight loop on the forward cast combined with a very fast haul.

HOW TO CONTROL THE LINE ON THE SHOOT

A basic mistake that most saltwater fly fishermen make is to let go of the line on the final forward cast. You shouldn't drop the line unless you just want to throw the fly as far as you can to get a long retrieve. Instead, you want to control the line on almost all casts.

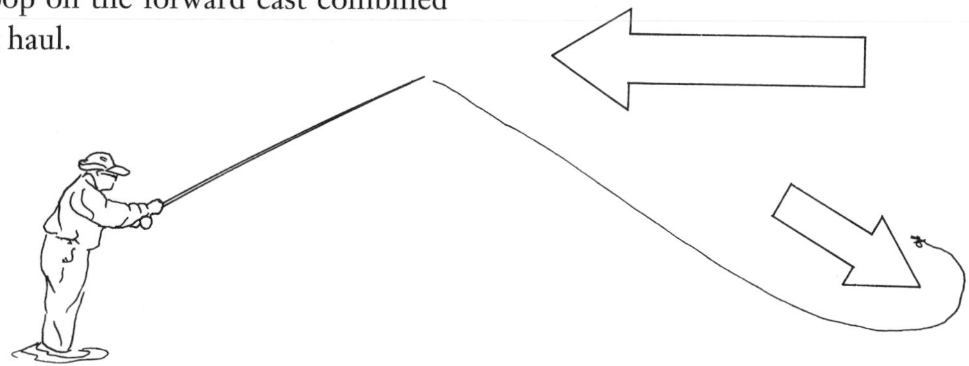

There are several reasons for this. If you fish for redfish, tarpon, permit, or bonefish on a skiff in the flats, you'll often have trouble seeing the fish. Your guide will be able to see the fish much more clearly from his or her elevated position on the platform. If you cast to a fish but let go of the line, you'll have to look down to recover the fly line to begin the retrieve. Once you've got the fly line, you look back again to locate the fish. It may take several precious moments to locate it, or you may never find it again, and the chance will disappear.

Another important reason that you need to control the line on the shoot is distance accuracy. Let's say you are casting to white hole on a flat, or to a jetty, or even a fish. Make an elevated cast that would travel well beyond the desired target. Instead of releasing the line, form a guide with the thumb and first finger around the line as it flows toward the target. When the fly is over the target, simply trap the line between the two fingers. Think about it—a spin fisherman makes a longer than needed cast, and then slows the lure by feathering the line with the forefinger. The line is trapped as the lure hovers over the target. The plug caster does the same thing with the thumb on the spool. Yet, most fly fishermen throw the fly out there and hope it lands where they want it.

Finally, if you control the line on the shoot, when the fly contacts the water, you can immediately begin a retrieve or set the hook should a fish strike. Fortunately, it's easy to learn how to control the line.

Make the final forward cast so that it travels upwards.

Curl the thumb and finger around the line as it flows toward the target. Watch the fly and close your thumb and finger when the fly arrives at the target.

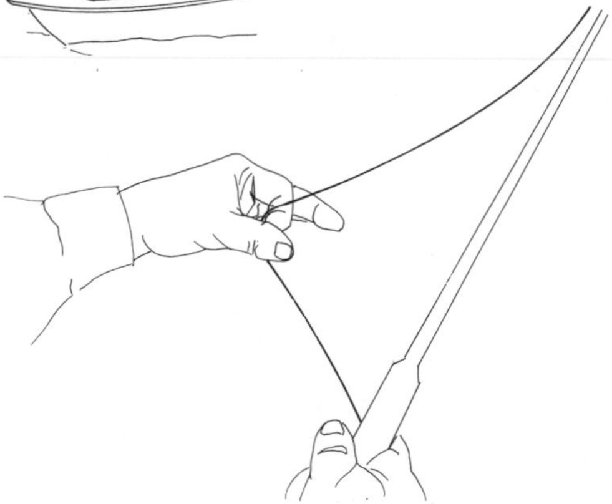

THE CHANGE OF DIRECTION CAST

One of thc most frustrating situations you can have as a flats fisherman is to see a fish when you're already retrieving your fly from a completely different direction. You need to cast to that fish, and to do this you need the change of direction cast. Most anglers change directions by making several false casts, which takes too much time and may spook the fish.

The most efficient way to make any forward cast is to set up the backcast 180 degrees from the target. If the backcast isn't directly opposite the target, much of the final forward cast's energy is wasted in redirecting the line. That's why most anglers have to make several false casts before getting the fly to the target. To make a quick change of direction cast, the first step is to direct the backcast so that it is opposite the target.

Lower the rod so the tip is near the surface and remove all slack from the line.

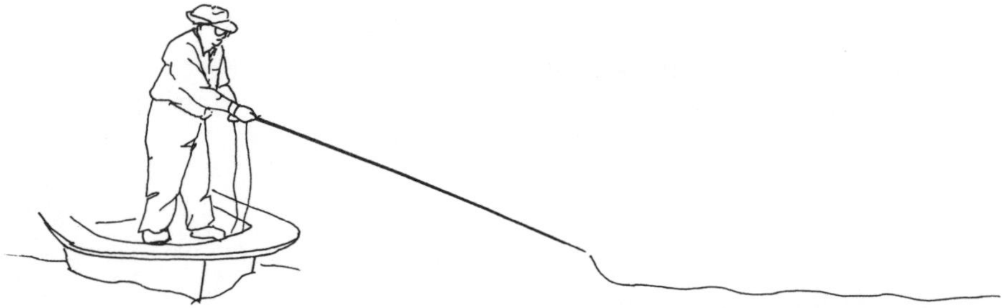

Move the rod tip in the direction of the target with a constant motion and with the rod tip very close to the water. You don't have to move it fast, but you can't stop. If you stop, you won't be able to make a backcast until you move the end of the fly line again. Also, the higher you raise the rod tip above the surface, the less efficient the backcast. Continue to sweep the rod to the side until the rod is pointing directly at the target. Many anglers make the backcast before they point it at the target, which makes the forward cast difficult.

When the rod is pointing at the target, make a strong backcast. Use a haul to assist the back and forward casts.

This useful cast is easy to learn and enables you to change directions within seconds, but it's difficult to perform at distances of 40 feet or more.

AVOIDING THE OTHER CASTER

When two right-handers or two left-handers are in a boat and they try to cast at the same time, they stand a good chance of hitting each other as they cast. One of the anglers always has to throw his line between himself and his companion. This is especially bad if both anglers are throwing weighted lines and weighted flies. An easy cast can eliminate this problem and maybe even save a friendship or trip to the doctor.

Let's say we have two right-handers in the boat. When the caster on the bow finishes a retrieve, he'll prepare for the next backcast by removing all slack and with the rod held low.

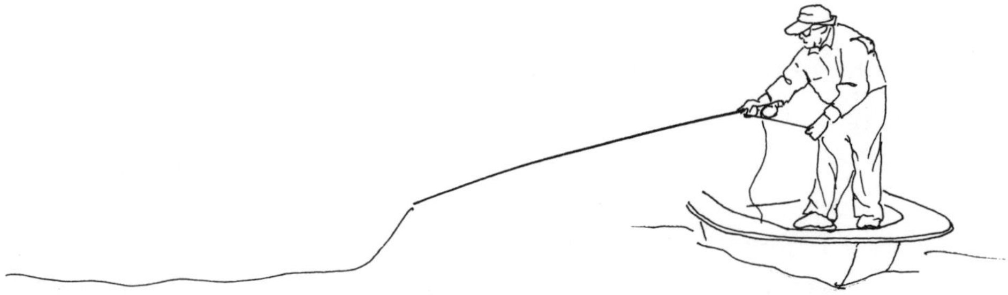

The angler faces the opposite direction from where he was previously retrieving, and prepares for a forward cast in that direction. He starts to load the rod as he starts to draw the rod across the surface. It is important to remember that the thumb should stay behind the rod handle.

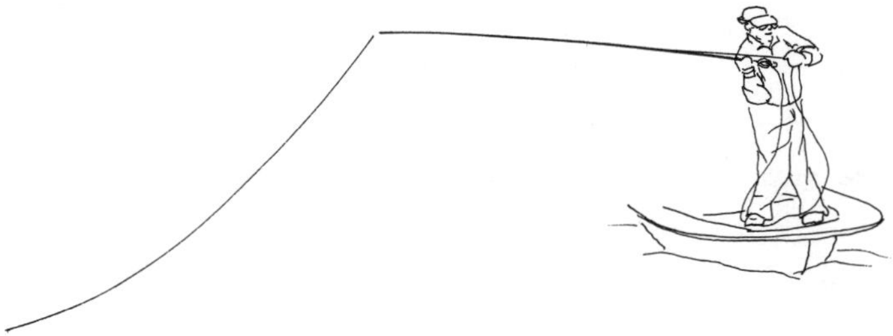

When the line is lifted from the surface, the angler makes a forward cast in the direction opposite his target.

As soon as the rod stops, the angler will lower the rod tip until it almost touches the surface. If you use a sinking line or heavy fly, don't let it fall below the surface or the next cast will be very difficult to make.

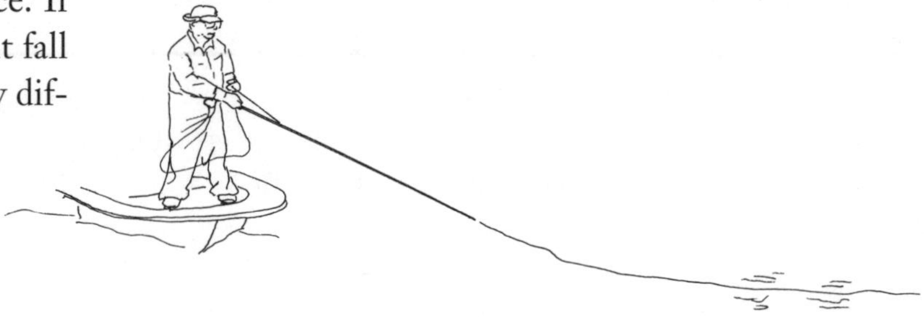

Now the angler turns his body, drags the fly line until the line leaves the water, and then makes the forward cast. After the forward cast, the angler can begin retrieving the fly. This cast can also be made to a fish that suddenly appears behind you while you are fishing in the opposite direction.

MAKING AN EXTRA EFFORT CAST

It's difficult to make a cast that is longer than ordinary, but it's especially difficult for anglers who cast fairly well. One mistake they tend to make is that they overpower the forward cast; but the main problem is the angle of the rod as it travels on the backcast.

The line always goes in the direction that the rod tip speeds up and stops, so if the angler brings the rod tip to a vertical position on the backcast, it will result in a poor backcast. The angler will be trying to lift a long line from the water, and after the line is off the surface, you need a powerful stroke to get this extra line behind the caster.

This is the conventional method most fly fishermen use when they pick up a longer-than-normal amount of line from the water.

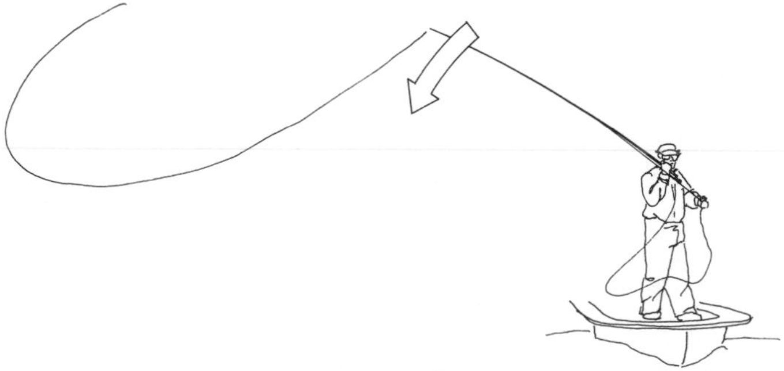

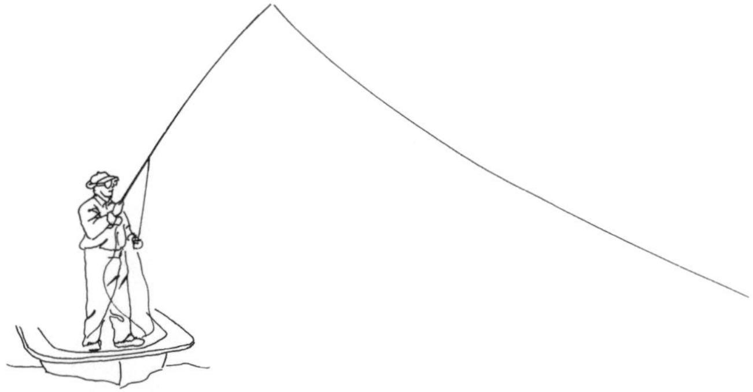

When the angler brings the rod up vertically and puts a lot of force in the backcast, it creates a deep sag in the line. On the stop portion of the speed-up-and-stop, the rod tip will dip back and down, so the line will also travel back and down, which creates even more sag, or slack. Remember that you can't make any cast until all slack is removed. When you make a forward cast with this much sag, you can't load the rod properly, so that much of the energy of the forward cast is wasted as you fight against this slack.

When making an extra effort cast, you need a fast, flat backcast with no sag. Begin by placing the rod tip close to the surface and removing all slack.

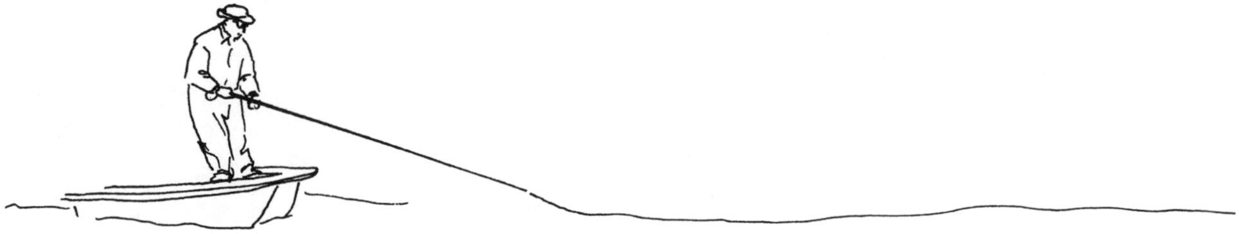

Make a sidearm backcast and imagine you are bringing the rod tip up a low ramp. The rod tip should be below the head as it continues up the ramp and passes the caster. There will be a sag in the cast if the rod tip rises above the height of the caster's head.

The backcast can be made at any time after the rod tip passes the angler, but it is crucial that the rod tip speeds up and stops as it rises. If the rod tip dips down on the speed-up or the stop, it will create sag.

Remember that the longer you can move a rod through the stroke, the easier it is to make the cast. If you raise the rod in a vertical position for an extra effort cast, you restrict how far back you can extend the rod. By starting low and "coming up the ramp," you can take the rod back as far as you can reach.

TWO WAYS TO MAKE A SPEED CAST

When fishing from a flats boat, you stand on the bow while your fishing partner or guide poles the boat toward the fish, and you have to be ready to

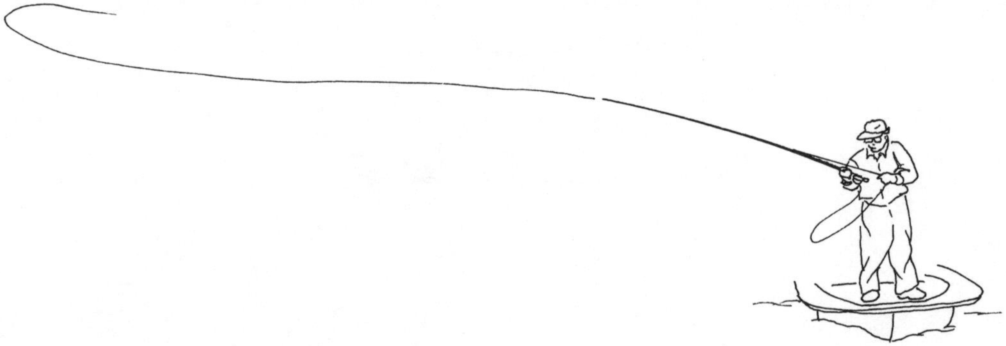

make a cast at all times. This requires that you have the line ready to fire, but you can't let the line fall overboard because it will snag on the bottom or on vegetation in the water.

First, you have to strip the amount of line you anticipate you'll need and no more. Extra line on the deck gets in the way, gets underfoot, or tangles. When you pull line from the reel, you'll build up a small pile of line at your feet or in your stripping basket. The rear of the line will be on top of that pile and the front of the line will be at the bottom. If you try to make a quick cast with the line in this condition, the line will feed from the bottom of the pile and tangle. So after you strip the line from the reel, cast the line out and retrieve the line back in. This will place the front of the line on the top of the pile, so when you make a quick cast, the line will feed from the top of the pile.

Speed Cast Number One: This is the easiest way to learn how to hold a measure of line and leader outside the guides, which allows you to cast quickly. Pull about a rod length of line outside the rod tip and pinch the fly between the thumb and first finger of your rod hand. The line should rest in your line hand. When you see a fish, lower the rod tip to the surface in the direction of the fish. Make an extra hard backcast in the opposite direction of the fish. Do not release the fly. Instead, keep it pinched just tightly enough so that the line

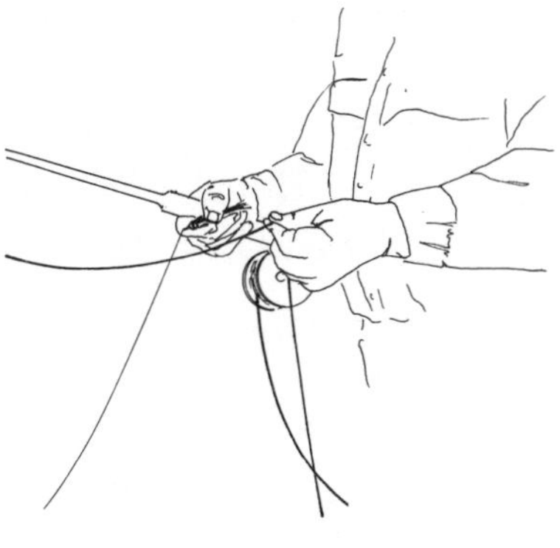

can pull it from your fingers. If you pinch the fly correctly, the rod will bend and load before the fly comes free. You'll harm the backcast if you drop the fly because the rod will have very little to pull against.

Once you make the backcast, you can false cast to get enough line out to reach the fish.

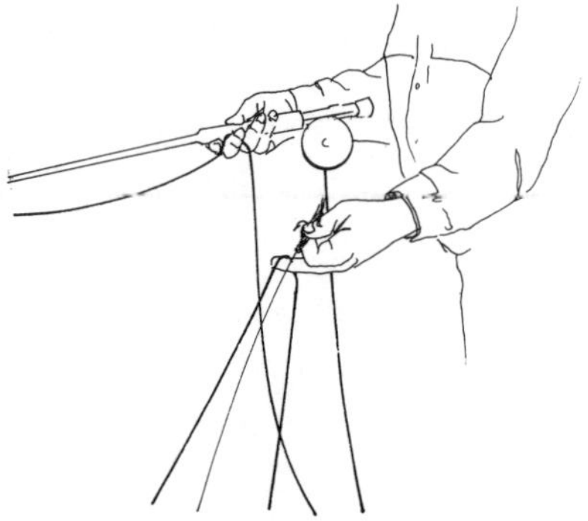

Speed Cast Number Two: This cast requires a little more practice, but it will allow you to put extra line in the air on the first backcast. There is a decided advantage in this. You'll often see a fish a few yards from the boat as you're poling around. With the first speed cast, you would need to make several false casts. But with speed cast number two, you can get a fly to a fish at least 25 to 30 feet away with a single backcast.

Pull almost two rod lengths of fly line outside the tip and pinch the fly between the thumb and forefinger of *the line hand* (instead of the rod hand, as in speed cast number one). Drape the fly line over your middle finger at a point about three feet from the leader butt, as illustrated. Do not grip the line on your middle finger—just allow it to drape across the finger. The rod hand traps the line under the *second* finger, as shown in

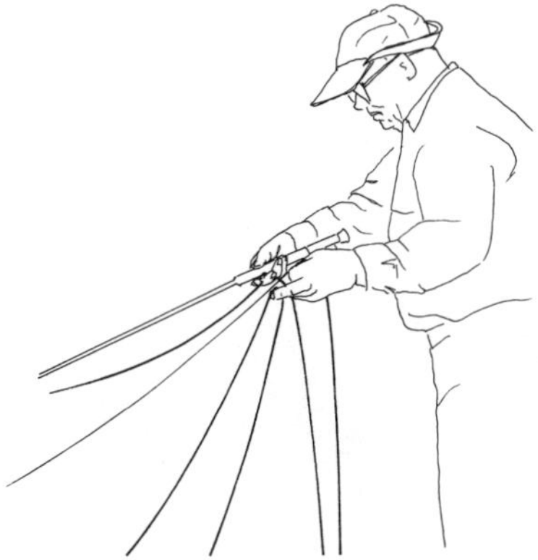

the drawing. The rest of the line can be safely stored on the deck.

When you see a fish, drop the tip to the surface in the direction of the fish. The longer the rod can sweep back, the easier the cast. Continue to pinch the line with your rod hand's middle finger just firmly enough so that the line has to pull it from your fingers. This aids in loading the rod for the backcast.

When you first learn this cast, you may make a forward cast before recovering the line in your line hand on the second backcast. The drawing

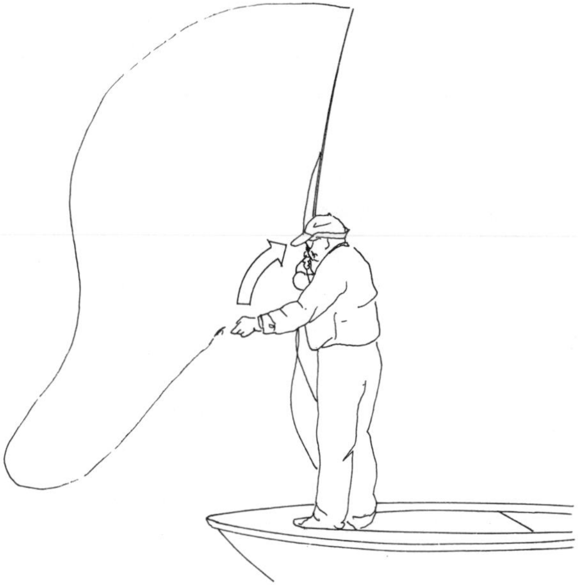

shows how to catch the line on the first backcast, which is most desirable. As the fly is torn from your fingers and the rod is moving back, reach up and grasp the line just in front of the rod handle.

If you trapped the line under the second finger of your rod hand, there will be ample room for you to catch the line with the other hand. If you clamp the line under the first finger of the rod hand, the line will be difficult to grasp because it will be right up against the rod.

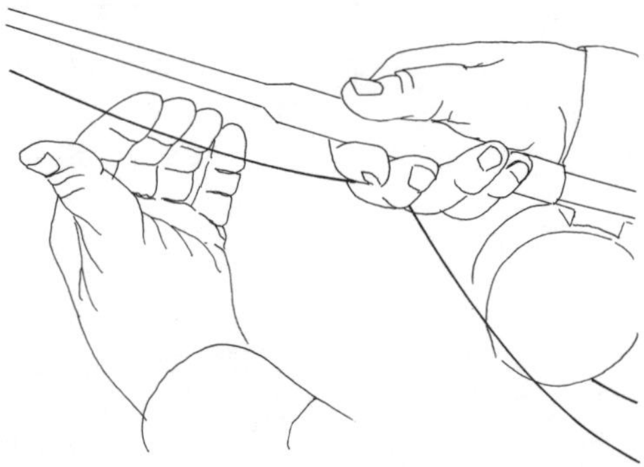

The line is now under control as you complete the backcast.

Now make the forward cast. A haul on the forward cast will help you get extra distance.

CASTING WEIGHTED FLIES AND LINES

Most fishermen agree that casting weighted lines or lead-core shooting heads is a frustrating and disagreeable task. They fear the possibility of getting hit with a heavy weighted line or a weighted fly, or of breaking their rod. If you are unaccustomed to them, casting with weighted lines or shooting core heads requires a lot of extra effort. As a result, many anglers avoid them, and even use floating lines when they know they would do far better with a sinking type.

Saltwater fly fishermen should actually use sinking lines more often than floating lines. Although Florida, the Bahamas, Christmas Island, and similar other saltwater fly-fishing hotspots offer shallow-water flats fishing, most anglers seek quarry closer to home. Local waters may be deep or there may be several channels with interesting possibilities. Whether you're fishing for kelp bass in California, salmon off Oregon and Washington, bluefish near the Outer Banks of North Carolina, or stripers off Nantucket, you need to get the fly well below the surface in order to fish effectively. Even with weighted flies, it's difficult to get to a fish that is more than five or six feet deep when using a floating line.

Another occasion for using sinking lines would be when you're fishing from the beach. Floating lines bob up and down on rough surf, which will make your retrieve erratic and unmanageable. It will also create slack between bobs, which may cause you to miss a strike. Even worse, the line remains on top and the fly can't get down near the bottom where the fish are.

With some species of fish, especially striped bass, the largest fish are almost always concentrated below the smaller ones in a school. Experienced striper fishermen have learned that when the fish are breaking, they should use a fast sinking line with a weighted fly. They'll cast into the melee, allow the line and fly to sink well below the frantic surface action, and are rewarded by catching the larger fish on the bottom. This also holds true when bluefish are breaking on the surface. In many situations, big seatrout lurk below the bluefish and feed on the bait that the bluefish destroyed.

Additionally, no line can cast into the wind—nor can a lead-core shooting head or a weighted line because they are thin and heavy, and when you learn how to properly throw a weighted line, it is the easiest of all lines to cast. The problem is that fishermen try to cast a weighted line the same way they cast a floating line, and they get in trouble on the backcast. Floating lines slow down at the end of the backcast, so instructors teach fly fishermen to rapidly accelerate the rod tip to keep the floating line traveling fast throughout the backcast. When you backcast a weighted line like a floating line and get it moving at high speed, the inertia keeps the fly moving. When the angler makes a forward cast, the heavy line has to make a sudden 180-degree turn and go the other way. This quick change in direction causes the most problems.

When casting a floating line, you want to make a fast backcast with a tight loop so that you maintain the necessary speed. It is just the opposite when casting a weighted line. You want to make a backcast with a wide loop so that you avoid the abrupt change of direction. The analogy I like to use is that the backcast should travel somewhat like a boat trailer attached to a car. When the car rounds a curve, the trailer should follow behind smoothly.

The first problem is that the line must be lifted to the surface before a backcast can be made. If you are fishing with a lead-core shooting head or sinking line, you need to retrieve until the rear of the sinking portion is at the rod tip. The thinner shooting line is not stiff enough to lift this heavy line. Once you've the retrieved the correct amount of line, make a roll cast. If the roll cast did not lie out in front of you, you need to make another roll cast. Never make a false cast with sinking lines or heavy flies to avoid a quick change in direction.

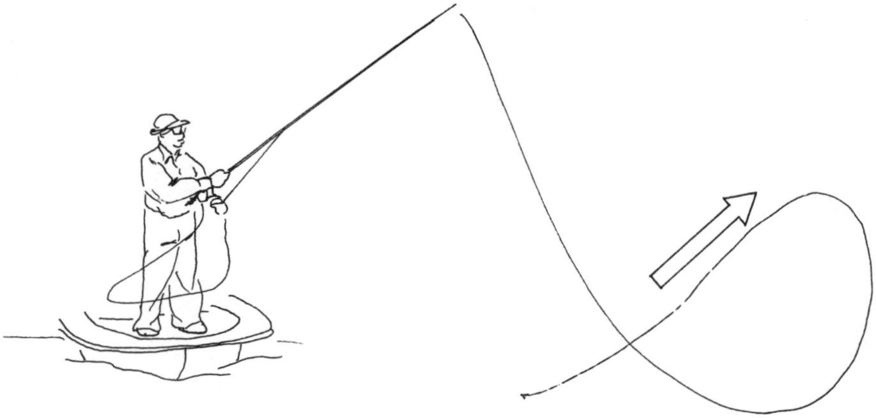

Watch the line end at the end of the roll cast. When it unrolls on the water it is time for step two. You can't wait too long, or the line will sink too far below the surface and you will need to make another roll cast. But if you move the rod tip to the rear as soon as the front end of the line strikes the water, even with a lead-core shooting head, it will remain close to the surface.

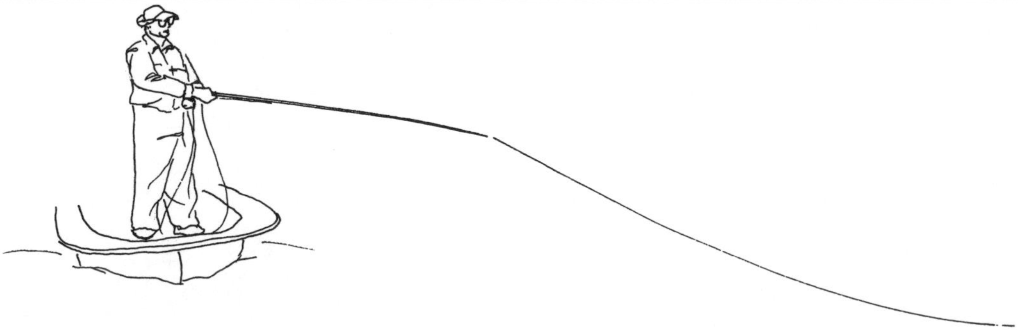

Keep the rod tip low as if you were making a low side cast and slowly draw the rod and line back. Be sure to keep your elbow hanging straight down. If you raise the elbow, you will have difficulty with the forward cast. When the rod is about 45 degrees in front of you, start to make a backcast with a wide loop. Continuously pull the rod tip around a curve. It's like pulling the rod tip inside a vertical horseshoe. You have to pull all the way around the horseshoe. This will make a wide loop and eliminate any quick change in direction from backcast to forward cast.

Once the backcast is ended, make a higher than normal forward cast with a gentle stroke and haul. If you apply too much force on the forward cast, you'll cause destabilizing shock waves through the line, wide loops, and loss of control. You'll get a longer cast by shooting the line at a higher angle.

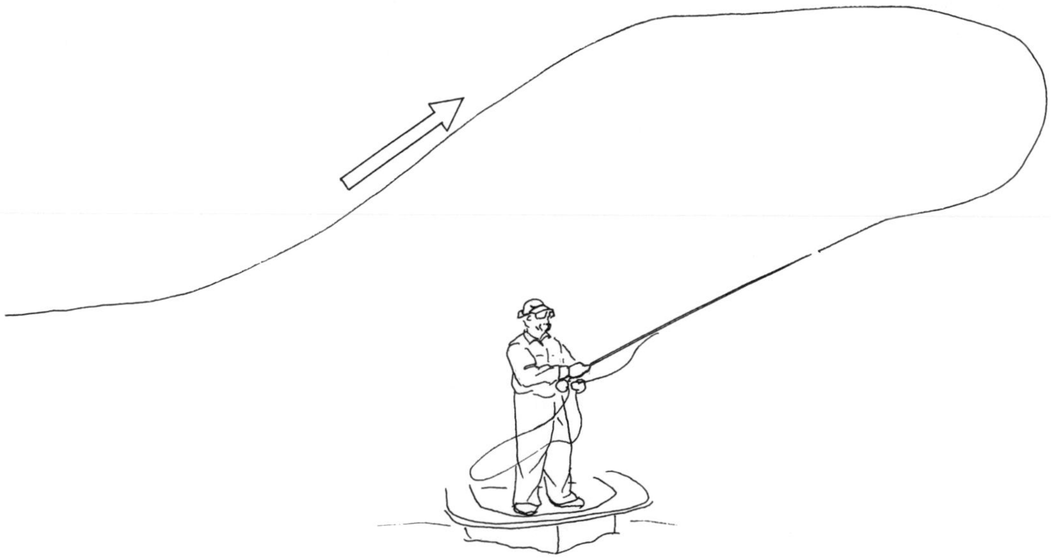

THE CURVE CAST

If you see a fish close by that is facing away from you and you cast beyond the fish, the fly will come toward the fish as you retrieve it. To the fish, this looks like the fly is attacking it, and the fish will generally refuse the fly. If you cast a fly in front of a fish while it is nearby and facing you, you'll pull the fish toward you during the retrieve. When the fish sees you it will spook. If you use a curve cast in these situations, you can present the fly to the fish, and retrieve the fly away from you and away from the fish. The curve cast can also be helpful when you want to throw a line around an obstruction or when you want to retrieve the line perpendicular to the shore instead of parallel to the shore and toward you.

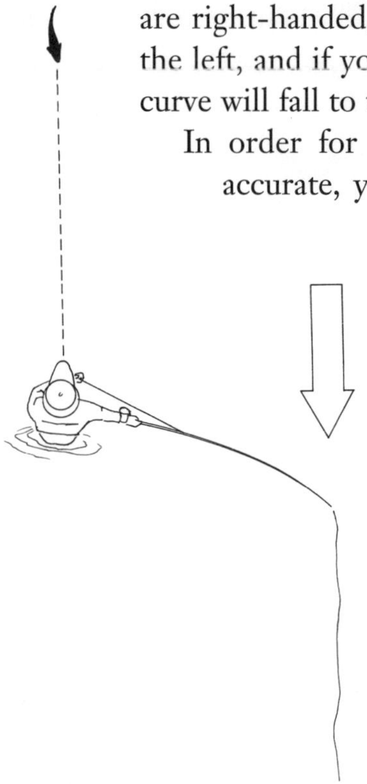

The curve cast is easy to learn. If you are right-handed, the curve will fall to the left, and if you are left-handed, the curve will fall to the right.

In order for the curve cast to be accurate, you must face the target. You should make the lowest backcast possible; you can't make a curve cast with a vertical backcast.

Keep the rod parallel to the surface of the water as you sweep it forward. Then, while still facing the fish, stop the rod abruptly at 45 degrees. The line will go in the direction that the rod tip speeds up and stops. If you make a very abrupt stop, the rod tip will curve to the left and the line will do the same. To make a bigger curve, stop the rod tip faster and more abruptly and haul the line. When most people first try the curve cast they don't make the speed-up-and-stop parallel to the water. Instead, the rod tip dives slightly toward the surface, so the line dives to the surface. To hone your skills, make the speed-up-and-stop at a climbing angle and bring it down with each practice cast.

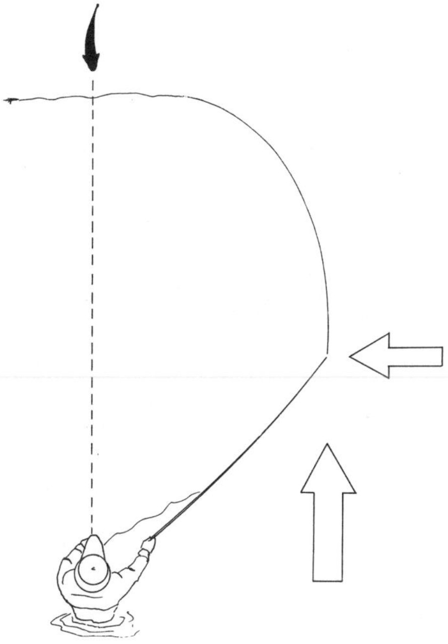

4

Other Helpful Tips

KEEPING THE LINE OUT OF TROUBLE

When fly fishing in salt water, managing your fly line is of paramount importance at all times. If you're wading and you trail the line behind you, the line can tangle in floating grass or other debris, or you can step on it, or the line can get tangled between your legs. All of these problems make it impossible to cast when and where you need to. You must also be ready to cast at all times while on the platform of a flats skiff or cruising on an offshore boat. To do this the line must be stored at a ready position, but you can only hold so much line outside the rod tip before it drags on the water, where it will surely catch on something and spoil the opportunity. You can't store this additional line on the deck of the boat because breezes tend to snarl the line into a twisted mess, and because it's easy to step on the line, get tangled with other objects in the boat, or otherwise foul the cast. Fishermen everywhere have lost thousands of opportunities to hook up because they were unable to manage their line. Fortunately, there are several methods and devices to avoid these problems.

Belly stripping basket: Several containers have been developed over the years to store the fly line prior to the last forward cast. They are termed stripping baskets (although none of them are actually baskets). The most commonly used is the belly stripping basket, which is held in position by a belt. I recommend a wide belt inserted twice through the basket to give it more stability. Most belts or straps have a quick-release button. Many anglers make such a basket from a plastic dishwashing pan, available in grocery stores, and attach 5-6 inch-long upright stubs of 100-pound test monofilament material along the bottom of the pan at 3 to 4 inch intervals. These allow the line to fall into the bottom of the basket in loose coils when you strip the line in, and allow the line to flow freely from the basket as you feed line to

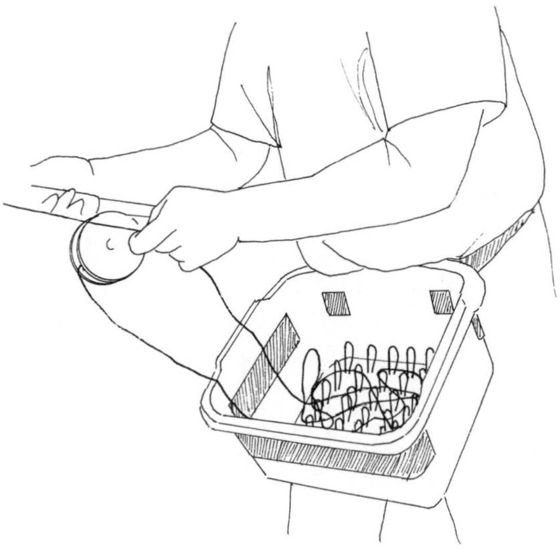

the rod when casting. My favorite stubs are plastic cable ties.

You'll also want to make a series of drain holes in the bottom and sides for any water that gets in the basket. Some anglers also attach closed cell foam around the upper edge of the basket as flotation so that the basket will float if they get into deep water.

Hip-style shooting basket: My favorite is the hip-style shooting basket because it allows freer movement during the retrieve. The opening is about the same size as the common dishpan basket, but the depth is about one foot, and it can be made from an ordinary plastic wastebasket by cutting off some of the top. As with the belly basket, make sure it has several large holes on the bottom to allow water to drain when you use it on the beach. I use cable ties in the base to hold the line in position.

I prefer the hip basket because when you bend over—to land a fish, for instance—the line in a belly basket will often spill out in front of you. This isn't a concern with the hip-style basket because it's deeper and because it's situated below the belt. The hip-style basket is also more comfortable and secure than the belly basket because it's held in position by two straps. The first is a shoulder strap, and the second is a strap that encircles the leg, holding it securely in place. This allows you to run along the beach or move around a boat without spilling line. So far as I know, there is no commercial hip-style stripping basket, but they're easy to make.

The Stalker: Fly fishermen lose hundreds of opportunities when they wade after a fish. The line often drags behind and catches on the bottom, coral, or sea grass, and the angler has to make several false casts just to get enough line out to make a presentation. Long casts are usually

unnecessary when you're wading the flats and sight fishing. The Stalker by Pro-Trim is a superb and inexpensive line management tool for such work. It has a clip so that you can hang it on your belt, and is designed to carry about 40 feet of line for instances where you only expect to cast less than 50 feet.

The Stalker is not a conventional stripping basket because it's designed only for wading; if you wade with the line hanging out, the line stands a good chance of getting caught on something. When fishing with The Stalker, you take the line out of The Stalker as soon as you spot a fish, then cast as usual. On the retrieve you drop the line to the surface. The Stalker and drop it to the surface near you. Once the game is over, you make a cast and then carefully store the line back in The Stalker before moving on. This allows you to manage your line and you can move around with greater ease than with a belly basket or hip basket. It's available from many fly shops or by calling Pro-Trim at 1-800-421-2586.

The Line Tamer: No matter how careful you are, a fly line can get into more trouble than you can imagine. In a boat the wind can push the line overboard, or the line can tangle and get underfoot. My van couldn't hold the number of fish I've lost as a result of stepping on the line or by snagging it on the rod holders, cleats, and baggage of a flats skiff. One of the best developments in years for boat anglers is another device by Pro-Trim called The Line Tamer.

This cylindrical container resembles a short smokestack with a stout base. The angler stands directly behind The Line Tamer, makes a cast, and retrieves the line into the container. That way, some of the line is in the container, ready for a cast. By casting and then retrieving the line into The Line Tamer before casting to a fish, you also

make sure that you're feeding line from the top of the line pile in The Line Tamer. If you simply stripped line off the reel into The Line Tamer, the line you would feed to the rod on your next cast would come from the bottom of the line pile, which may cause tangles. Also, it's wise to strip a little more line than you think you'll need. If you shoot all the line in The Line Tamer and then begin the retrieve, you have to make sure it is dropping inside the container, which may cause distraction at a crucial moment. If you've left some line inside, there is no problem. As you make your retrieve, you just strip line normally and let it fall into the container. If you have to change casting direction, simply change the position of the canister.

The device has several other benefits. For instance, some lines tend to stick together; when using monofilament with a shooting head, the fast-traveling head will tend to lift all the lighter mono toward the guides in a snarl. You can eliminate this problem by adding a bit of water to the bottom of The Line Tamer.

Also, if you're fishing a flat and you make a run to another spot, you have to wind in the line, and when you get to the next place, you have to strip off line, and make a cast before you are ready. That's not a problem with The Line Tamer. Secure the line against the rod with a rubber band or a Velcro strap (supplied with the unit) and place the rod, reel, and line in The Line Tamer. When you arrive at the next place, you can release the rubber band or Velcro strap, pick up the rod, and be ready for your next cast in just a few seconds.

It's also a good idea to have two Line Tamers when flats fishing. You may be fishing for redfish when a shark or tarpon shows up. Then you frantically try to get rid of the redfish outfit and strip out line for the correct rig. But this almost never works, of course. If you have two Line Tamers, you can have two ready-to-cast outfits.

Put the Line in Your Belt or In Your Pocket: If you're being poled around on a flats skiff and don't have a Line Tamer handy, don't hold the fly in one hand and let the line between the reel and the stripping guide on the rod go

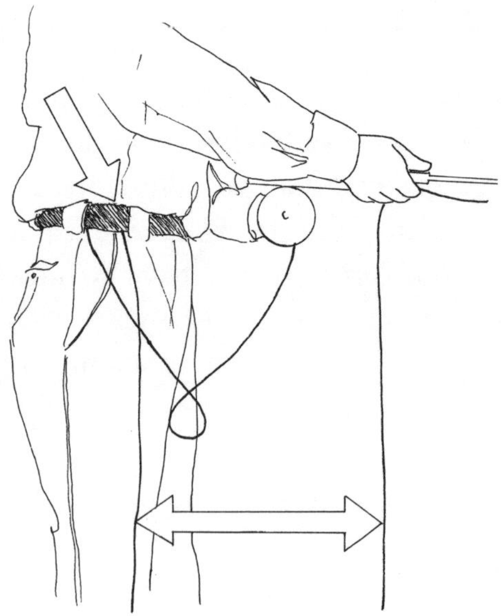

slack. You'll have a lot of line out between the rod tip and your fly while the forefinger of your rod hand will hold down the slack line between the reel and the stripping guide. When a slight breeze picks up all the loose line hanging around, the two lines will get twisted together, which makes any casting impossible.

You can eliminate tangles between these two lines by taking about 18 inches from the reel and tucking it under your belt, as shown in the drawing. Now the two lines will be separated and the line under your belt will slip off easily when you cast. If you don't have a belt, you can also tuck a bit of the line in an empty pocket, as illustrated.

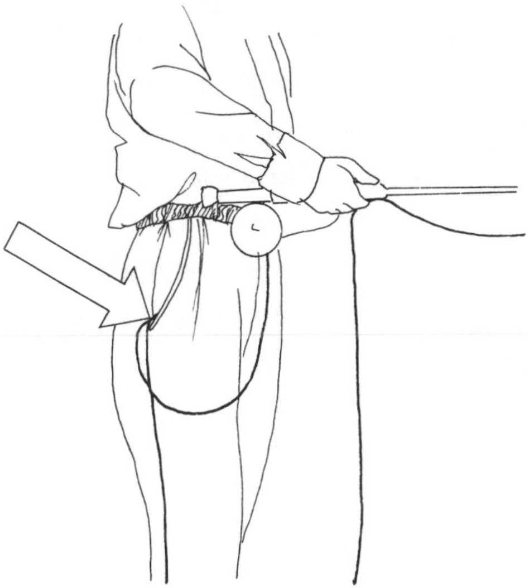

Stand Upwind of Your Fly Line: Fly fishermen can't figure out how they come to stand on their line while standing perfectly still on the bow of a flats boat. When an angler stands downwind of his or her line, the subtle breezes and motions of the boat constantly push the line toward their feet. If the sole of the angler's foot lifts a bit as the boat rocks or they change positions, the line will get underfoot and spoil the angler's casts.

Always stand upwind of the fly line. If the boat changes direction, then you need to change where your feet are positioned. While not foolproof, if you're constantly aware of the position of your feet, the wind, and your line, you'll stand a better chance of not spoiling your cast.

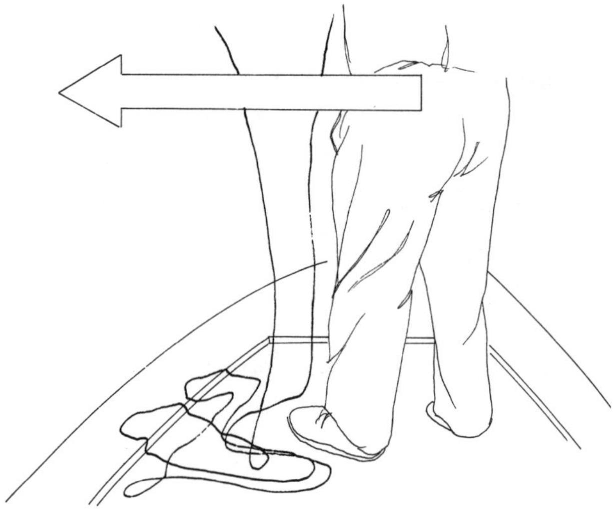

Store Line Off of the Casting Platform: Fly fishermen in a flats skiff tend to stand at the very tip of the bow while they look for fish or cast to them. When they make a cast and retrieve the fly, they strip the line back directly on to their feet, which causes a tangled mess.

The ideal flats skiff would have a small, elevated forward platform with a larger platform where you could place line immediately behind it. Since no such skiff exists, we have to make do with what is available. If you stand near the rear of the casting platform and drop line to the deck beyond the platform as you retrieve it, you'll reduce the chance of standing on it. Just be sure to clear the lower deck space of line-tangling objects.

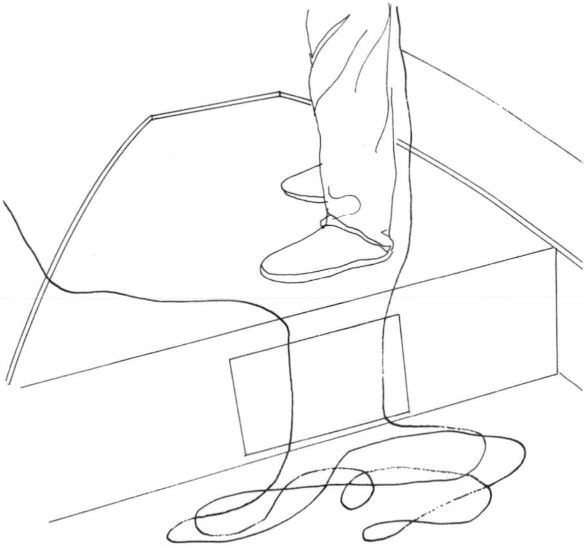

Use Netting: Most boats have several different fixtures and objects that snag fly line, and if you don't have a Line Tamer, fine mesh netting can offer a simple and inexpensive solution. Many commercial fishing supply houses sell ¼ or ⅜-inch mesh netting; a common minnow seine works well, also. Ideally, the netting should be approximately 7 feet by 7 feet, though slightly smaller nets will suffice.

The minnow seine is usually 4 feet by 7 feet. I like to remove the floats on one end and add several small sinkers to each side of the netting. The breeze will blow through the netting and the sinkers will hold it in place over motors, tackle boxes, or whatever may get in the way. You'd be surprised how much it helps your casting, and one advantage it holds over the Line Tamer is that you

can transport it with ease. The Line Tamer can be difficult to transport to distant areas, but netting takes up virtually no room and has saved the day in remote fishing locations.

Get Rid of Your Shoestrings: Much of the line you intend to shoot to the target lies at or near your feet. If you have protruding shoe-strings, they may catch your line and ruin your cast. Moccasins are perhaps the absolute worst shoes you can wear because the leather laces stick well out and almost certainly catch your fly line.

Fortunately, there is a simple solution. Purchase some 3/8-inch wide elastic at a drug store or sewing outlet and remove the shoestrings from your tennis shoes. Lace the elastic through the shoe by starting at the top and ending at the toe of the shoe. If the shoe has small eyelets, I cut a taper on the elastic and pull it through with a pair of hemostats or needlenose pliers. Put the shoe on your foot, adjust the elastic until it is comfortably snug, and tie the elastic off with a secure square knot. To ensure that the elastic

never comes loose, I like to place a drop of Cyanoacrylate glue on the knot. In addition to being more fly-casting friendly, your shoes will also be more convenient. Instead of having to tie them, all you do is slip your foot inside.

DON'T USE A LONG-BILLED HAT

Most anglers aren't aware that they monitor the line throughout its flight to the target, but we've all had the experience of realizing that a cast is bad and stopping it in midflight. I mention this because we do look at our line in flight, and how we look at the line has a lot to do with how accurately we place the fly.

Some fly fishermen wear a hat with an extended brim, which impairs accuracy. The long brim obscures the line until it nears the target,

when it's too late to make the subtle changes that will result in a successful presentation.

The brim of a baseball hat (or slightly shorter at a maximum of about 3⅕ inches) is the best brim length. This length is long enough to shade the eyes but not so long that it interferes with monitoring the line.

The color of the underside of the brim also affects accuracy. If the brim has a bright underside, the sunlight reflected from the water bounces off the light underside and impairs your vision. A dark underside will absorb the sunlight, allow you to see better, and reduce eyestrain.

CASTING ETIQUETTE

While saltwater fly fishermen often wade, most saltwater fly fishing occurs on a boat. As the angler, you'll usually stand in the bow of a flats boat while your guide or companion stands in the stern. When you or your partner see a fish, you must never cast directly ahead because you have a good chance of hooking your companion. Instead, allow your partner to pole the boat to the side so that your backcast will be over open water and will avoid the person in the rear of the boat.

BE PATIENT ON THE BACKCAST

One of the major reasons anglers don't hook up while fishing calm, shallow water is that they lift line abruptly from the surface on the backcast. The scenario is that the angler makes a cast to a fish, but perhaps the fish doesn't see the fly, rejects the fly, or changes direction. The angler then has to make another presentation. But keep in mind that floating line is held on the water by surface tension. If the angler makes a backcast with even a foot of the line still on the surface, the line will rip off the surface and spook the fish. Always lift all of the fly line from the surface, gently, before you make another backcast. This is a major factor in whether or not you catch bonefish. Bonefish and permit flies are usually weighted, so when false casting, make sure that the fly doesn't dip down and strike the water in front of the boat while false casting.

WEAR CLEAN SHOES

Shoes with deep cleats such as most hiking and running shoes collect huge amounts of dirt. That's especially true when walking down a beach to get into a boat. If you step into a boat in the

Florida Keys with dirty shoes the guide is liable to have a heart attack—or to give you one. You may think the guide is overreacting, but he's not. The fly line will pick up any grit or dirt on the deck. This will restrict casting distance, wear out lines, and deteriorate rod guides. Any line should always lie on a clean deck. Often a guide will insist (and correctly so) that you step on a wet towel and wipe your feet clean before entering the boat. If the shoes are not perfectly clean they will leave grit and dirt on the deck. Alternatively, the guide may direct you to remove your shoes.

FLY-LINE COLOR AND DESIGN

Manufacturers now make lines that are designed for either tropical or cooler temperature use. A striped bass line will generally perform poorly in warmer climates, and a bonefish line will be just as bad in colder climates such as New England. If you fish the tropics or Florida, a dark line will pick up a great deal of heat lying on the deck and cast like a wet noodle. For tropical, sunny climates use a light-colored or clear line.

EXERCISES TO IMPROVE ACCURACY

As I've said before, saltwater fly presentation needs to be fast but also accurate. There are two fun things you can do to improve your accuracy, reduce your loop size, and generally make you a better caster. Buy a standard Hula Hoop and tape it to a clean pole with the bottom of the loop about 4 feet off the ground. Try to throw a cast through the loop at a distance of about 25 feet.

You probably won't be able to do this at first, but as you practice and concentrate on forming the loop, it will slowly decrease in size until you'll be able to throw most of your casts through the loop. Step back a little farther and repeat the exercise. When you can throw at least six out of ten loops through the hoop at 40 feet, your technique will have improved substantially.

A mouse trap is another fun tool to improve accuracy. Get a mouse trap with a bait pan at least an inch wide. Cock the trap and cast a weighted fly with the bend and point removed from a distance of about 25 feet. Your initial inaccuracy will probably embarrass you at first, but as you concentrate on the trap you'll get closer and closer. When you can hit the trap in one cast out of ten, and the rest of your casts land within 6 inches of the target, you'll find that your overall accuracy has improved dramatically.

CONCENTRATE ON THE TARGET

Finally, many anglers are amazed when they see a good fly fisherman shoot a fly into a tiny hole in a shoreline brush. If you watch a marksman shoot a pistol, they often bring the pistol up, fire quickly, and hit the target dead-on. The reason they're able do this is because their bodies instinctively point the gun at the target, and because they keep their focus on the target. When applied to fly fishing, focus on that tiny hole in the bushes instead of the entire bush.

INDEX